Create a Business-Busting Partnership with Your

Assistant—The Executive's Guide

*Susie Barron-Stubley*

ISBN 978-1-291-14108-5

## *Dedication*

For all of the Executives and Assistants who have held complete disregard for the established boundaries and the historical undertones of the role of the EA and have driven the professional partnership into an influential and respected business alliance. I salute you.

# Table of Contents

# Foreword

Having a great working relationship with my EA has, without a doubt, made my own role as Diesel Managing Director for the UK much more rewarding and successful. Many of the passages in this book were read with a wry smile and a wistful and nostalgic look on my face as I recalled my own journey when I first joined Diesel in late 2008.

After 16 years in a very large American company, where dedicated EA roles were few and far between, indeed, despite being promoted to 'associate director' I had always had to share the privilege with others, I joined Diesel and began working for the first time with my very own executive assistant, Jacqueline.

It was clear from the outset that she had so much more to offer beyond the usual responsibilities and we set about trying to define a job content which would meet my needs, the organisation requirements and of course her own developmental ambitions. Simultaneously, we also started working on what kind of working relationship we wanted to have. How often should we meet? What was our preferred method of communication? How could we give each other constructive feedback in the right way so that our working relationship continued to improve? Nearly four years on and we are still working to maximise both her role and further refine our relationship. One constant shines through though: we have both grown and developed a strong partnership which makes coming to work an absolute pleasure.

What this book does is give you a perfect framework to ensure that with both the role and the relationship, you are both getting the most from each other and doing it in a way which will cut down on the awkward bits and difficult moments...we've all been there at some point!

So, regardless of which end of the partnership you occupy, enjoy this thoroughly straightforward and enjoyable read and then marvel at the way it can up the smile count and productivity rate at the same time. Invest now and the 'gold bar' returns will soon start kicking in!

Jonny Hewlett
Managing Director
Diesel UK Ltd
London

# Dear Boss,

Congratulations on being the lucky recipient of this book!

It may have landed on your desk as a birthday or Christmas present from your EA. Or she may have bought this book for you as a 'Welcome to Being My Boss' gift. Or it may be from a thoughtful colleague or boss who 'saw this and thought of you'.

Whatever the reason, you have been given this book because someone is serious about your working relationship with Your EA. Which makes you one very lucky Boss.

## A Little Note on the Assistant/EA/Job Title Thing...

Job titles are a tricky old business for Assistants and different areas of the world use different titles. Executive PA, PA, Business Assistant, Management Assistant, Corporate Assistant, Personal Assistant, EA, Executive Assistant, Administrative Professional...I could go on, but won't. For the purpose of this book I'm going to refer to Assistants as Executive Assistants— **EAs**—mainly to save ink. I will use this term to encompass all of the above job titles.

## What's This Book About?

For some years now I have been training EAs on how to develop an effective working relationship with their Bosses. And in these sessions, the most frequent phrase I hear is: 'That's all very well, but you need to tell it to my Boss'.

I always ask EAs the question, 'Do you feel well managed by your boss?' You may be surprised but the overwhelming response to this is a resounding 'No!' I'm as baffled as you as to why this might be. You're clearly good at managing huge budgets and global teams, so how come Your EA feels a little short-changed?

Having an EA is not simply about having someone to run all the boring bits of your life. Of course it's fabulous being able to go to a meeting in Antwerp without having to worry about how you'll get there. But is that all Your EA does for you? And what, when it comes down to it, do you do for her?

Your relationship with your EA is one of the most important professional relationships in your life: sure, Your EA isn't going to promote you. She's not going to give you a pay-rise and she's not going to put a word in to the Board on your behalf. But what she will do is ensure you're able to perform in a way that ultimately gets you those things.

## What Will You Get Out of It?

Work well with Your EA and you're likely to be happier, more productive and, ultimately, much, much better at your job.

This book will help you achieve the practically-perfect Nirvana of an EA/Boss working relationship. Through developing a solid framework and structure, you will learn how to:

1. Define the role of Your EA

2. Work successfully with Your EA

It will look at:

1. Management of the role (what you're doing together)

2. Management of the relationship (how you'll do it together)

The process is really simple and it's really straightforward. Nothing comes from nothing, so of course you'll need to put some work into it, but the process is tried and tested and gives the results you need: a brilliant working relationship with Your EA.

To perform effectively in your position, you need to use your EA just as effectively. She is your Business Partner and, I'm sorry to use this word so early on, but you have a responsibility to both of you to invest in that partnership so you're both running at the same speed.

This book may make you chuckle. It may make you think. But above all, it will give you a step-by-step guide to Getting It Right and all the joy and successes that comes with being part of a fantastic, enterprising, business-busting duo.

So, are you ready?

Let us begin...

*Susie*

**P.S.    *A Little Note on the He/She Thing...***

*Through my work I am, of course, aware that there are She EAs and He EAs. For ease, however, and because a significant imbalance remains and most EAs are still women, I have chosen to refer to EAs as 'she'. And while the bosses in my story are both male, I do not automatically assume that you are a male too. That is why I have used neutral gender in my process.*

# The Tale of Two Bosses—Part One: Two Bosses Get Two EAs

*This is the story of how two very different Bosses became so brilliantly efficient and productive that statues were erected in their honour and there are currently plans for a public holiday so that people may celebrate them suitably.*

Once upon a time, in an office far-far away there were two Bosses.

The Bosses both lived in the same Kingdom and were the best of friends. Each day they worked side-by-side as hard as they could, just as they always had since joining the Kingdom as Executives all those moons ago. And even though they each had twenty five Executives of their own now to boss, they always made time for one another.

That was until one day when the First Boss received an email from the Second Boss cancelling a lunch appointment.

He was too busy, he said.

Shrugging, the First Boss agreed that they were very busy and Second Boss was probably right. They had been discussing only the other day that the more responsibility the King gave them, the more hours they seemed to work. Indeed they had both caught the midnight train twice the previous week. Still, he thought, as his stomach rumbled, it was a shame they hadn't caught up as he had an idea he had wanted to run past the Second Boss before the next meeting with the King. Plus he really liked the salt beef sandwiches in the cafe.

But all of this was forgotten when one of First Boss's Executives stumbled into his office bearing mountains of files and much confusion.

The next day, First Boss and Second Boss were due to meet for lunch again. This time, First Boss had to cancel because he had so much work, thanks to the Executive with all the paper.

This went on and on and the Bosses began to see less and less of each other, even though their offices were only a hop, skip and a jump apart, and they were the only ones still there as the clock in the square outside chimed nine, ten, eleven o'clock at night.

Then one day the King, concerned that the First Boss had missed another meeting and that the Second Boss hadn't presented some papers on time again, summoned the two Bosses to his office.

'I have been thinking,' said the King. 'You two are working very hard and your teams have great respect for you, but I've noticed your individual productivity has dropped.'

'We have so much to do,' said First Boss.

'If we could have some help with our diaries or keeping track of where we are on our projects, maybe that would solve the problem,' said Second Boss.

The King hesitated and thought for a moment. 'I have it!' he suddenly said, leaping from his chair. 'I should have thought of this months ago!'

'What is it?' asked First Boss.

'I am going to give you each an EA,' said the King.

'An EA?' said the Bosses excitedly.

'Yes,' said the King. 'But you may only have an EA if you promise to use them wisely. EAs are magical beings and if you do not heed some simple rules, you will waste yours. And, as you know, wasting magic in our Kingdom is dangerous.'

'We promise!' exclaimed the Bosses. 'We promise!'

'Good,' said the King. 'Then EAs you shall have.'

'King?' stammered First Boss as he and Second Boss disengaged from a celebratory hug. 'What are the rules?'

'Ah,' said the King, smiling sagely. 'Now that you will need to work out for yourselves.'

And so the very next day, when the two Bosses clamoured to get out of the lift before everyone else and almost skipped towards their offices, barely daring to dream that what the King had offered them would be real, they saw what they had for so long been waiting for. Sitting at brand new desks before their doors were their very own EAs.

**Now all they had to learn was how to use them...**

# Introduction To The Process

There are two strands to a great working relationship:

- Management of the Role—*what* you're doing together.

- Management of the Relationship—*how* you'll do it together

Both are equally importance—an imbalance in either will mean a less productive outcome—yet it's not always easy to understand how one impacts on the other.

Following the process I lay out in the following two sections will give you the tools and understanding to create the ideal balance.

## The Investment Process

To get the EA you want will require investment from you. This investment will be, naturally, a time investment, but it will also require investment in the form of thought and energy.

I'm well aware how off-putting that can seem. I'm well aware that you have plenty of other pressing things which demand your time, thought and energy.

Likewise, I'm well aware of how loaded the word investment actually is.

**Because investment implies effort.**

You hear 'investment' and think of the hours you put into the last deal you worked on or report you delivered. You think of the investment required by the gym, and people come out of there after 'investing' looking half-dead.

However, like those occasions when you invest time in your work or on the bench-press, when you invest time, thought and energy in creating the kind of EA you want, you will get the result you want.

The amount of investment you make is up to you, but this process needs you to look at what your EA is doing and how you're working together. And while you're doing that, you need to think: really? Is that right? Is that enough? Is it what I want?

Investment is always about return. Which, of course you know, being the shrewd businessperson you are. But I suppose I'm saying that the difference between financial investment and investing in EAs is significant: when investing your money you *hope* to get at least your initial investment back.

If you invest in the role of Your EA, you are guaranteed a return.

**The Two-Headed Investment Beast**

I have broken the Investment Process down into two parts to match the two elements of the working relationship.

- Section One will look at **The Investment Part One:** *The Role*
- Section Two will look at **The Investment Part Two:** *The Relationship*

The aim is that you will work on both of the processes at the same time—they naturally fit together—and the goal is that once you've completed these processes you will be able to comfortably:

1.  Define the role of Your EA

2.  Work successfully with Your EA

By understanding both of these points, you will have the Holy Grail of EAs: an EA who is also your Business Partner.

There is no more powerful outcome from this process than that.

# The Tale of Two Bosses—Part Two: How The Bosses Learnt What An EA Isn't

That very morning the two Bosses set to work with their new EAs.

First Boss's EA had been an EA for a few years in another Kingdom. She had looked after a few Executives in the other Kingdom and had become a very good EA with very good experience. First EA had been asked to be the EA for First Boss because the King was sure she would do a fantastic job.

Second Boss's EA had been an EA for a few years in the same Kingdom. She had looked after a Big Cheese who had just retired and gone to sail boats in the great Oceans. Second EA had been asked to be the EA for Second Boss because the King was sure that she, too, would do a fantastic job.

As the clock struck one on that first afternoon, the two Bosses happened to bump into one another by the coffee machine.

'How is your EA?' asked First Boss, cautiously.

'Oh, marvellous!' exclaimed Second Boss. 'Just marvellous! She's changed my life!' He swirled his coffee. 'And yours?' Second Boss asked, breaking the silence that had fallen between them.

'Oh incredible!' exclaimed First Boss. 'Just incredible!' And then he too swirled his coffee and cleared his throat.

'So,' said Second Boss after a moment. 'What's your EA doing for you?'

First Boss shrugged. 'She's holding my coat,' he said. 'I saw it in a film once. A Boss walked into his office and his EA held his coat. It is actually quite convenient.'

Second Boss nodded and rubbed his chin, thoughtfully. 'Coat holding,' he said, approvingly.

'Yes,' said First Boss. 'She's very good at it, although she was looking a little tired when I came to get my coffee.'

'Maybe you should give her a chair?'

They both laughed heartily before taking big slurps of coffee.

'So,' said First Boss. 'What's your EA doing for you?'

'Well,' said Second Boss. 'I am quite relieved to be here with you now because we've been doing dictation all morning.'

'Dictation?' said First Boss, quietly impressed.

'Yes,' said Second Boss. 'I read it in a novel once that a character's EA was always taking dictation.'

'And how's that working out for you?'

Second Boss drained his coffee. 'To tell you the truth, I am exhausted,' he said. 'And I have not done any of my work. I ran out of reports to read out to her around twelve o'clock and I had to resort to the *Screw-Fix* catalogue.'

They both stood for a moment, lost in thought until First Boss finally spoke.

'I bought mine a gift this morning,' said First Boss.

'Me too!' said Second Boss.

'Thought it might make the first morning special,' said First Boss.

'Me too!' said Second Boss. 'What did you get your EA?'

'A nail file,' said First Boss. 'I see it all the time in films: EAs love to file their nails.'

'Me too!' said Second Boss. 'Me too! Did yours like it?'

First Boss hesitated. 'I am not sure,' he said, recalling the look of surprise on his new EA's face, which might have also been mixed with pleasure but might just as well have been mild offense.

'Me either.'

They stopped talking and stared at their coffee cups.

'I thought getting an EA would make my life easier,' said First Boss.

'Me too,' said Second Boss quietly. 'Me too.'

They both sighed and again slipped into silence.

Meanwhile, on the other side of the Kingdom, two brand new EAs were whispering in the coat cupboard.

'How's your first morning?' asked First EA rubbing her aching calves as she sat on a pile of coats.

Second EA shook her head sadly and flexed her right hand. 'Ridiculous,' she said. 'He had me writing out the dimensions of an array of circular saws.'

First EA looked surprised. 'I thought we dealt with...'

'I know,' said Second EA. 'I think he thought that was something we were supposed to do together. You know. Dictation.'

First EA rolled her eyes. 'I have been holding his coat since nine-thirty this morning,' she said and shook out her arms. 'If I had known that was all you needed to do as an EA, I wouldn't have put so much effort into that project management diploma.'

'I don't know,' said Second EA. 'I felt my graphic design skills were being well utilised writing down the serial numbers of screwdriver sets.' She rubbed her hand again. 'I think I invented a new font.'

They sighed together.

Above the silence in the cupboard First EA and Second EA could hear the slow, steady tick-tock of the big clock outside.

# Section 1: Managing The Role

The key to having a Great EA is knowing what Your Great EA does.

This section will outline the process which will help you clarify this.

We will look at the Investment Process and how this will assist you to develop and confirm the role of Your EA.

We will also look at identifying and developing boundaries and priorities. We will consider how to manage your expectations of Your EA, Your EA's expectations of herself, and her colleagues' expectations of her. We will also look at the benefits of allowing Your EA to assert herself effectively.

So let's take a look at the Investment Process: The Role.

# The Investment Part One—The Role

The process is made up of four points:

1. Planning
2. Developing
3. Implementing
4. Reviewing

## 1. Planning

To improve something you need to know what you want to improve. Do you know what Your EA actually does? Apart from the obvious? Do you know her job description?

This part of the process is where you're collecting information to review in the Developing section. During this time, you'll meet briefly with Your EA to explain what you're doing, ask her to join you in reviewing her role and reassure her that you're working together.

You will also spend a little bit of time thinking about who Your EA is and what her role is and then, finally, schedule a longer meeting with Your EA where you'll really get into what Your EA can and will be doing going forward.

## 2. Developing

Now that you have an understanding of what Your EA does and what she could be doing in the future, it is time to develop those thoughts into reality.

This part of the process is essentially one significant meeting; something I like to call the *Wipe The Slate Clean Meeting*. This is an opportunity for both of you to move away from what has gone before and begin from where you want to be.

At this meeting you will both clarify:

- The role of Your EA: its purpose and objectives
- How Your EA fits in with your role
- How Your EA fits in with the organisation
- Your EA's goals

This meeting will give you a new working method for you to apply together.

## 3. Implementing

Now comes the practical part where you communicate Your EA's boundaries and responsibilities to your colleagues, to ensure there are no compromises or awkward moments ahead for Your EA.

Then you both focus on applying the new plans to your every-day working lives.

## 4. Reviewing

As with anything new, you'll need to check-in over the next few weeks to make sure everything is going okay. Some things won't work like you wanted them to; others will be going like a dream. It's important you know which is which and can make changes or remove things altogether to avoid any complications.

Keep reviewing as you go to make sure you get what you want from Your EA.

### How Long Will This Take?

As you work your way through the following process, it is important to accept it will take time. Don't give up if it doesn't work straight away. It will if you both work together and that's what the Reviewing part is for.

Overall, remember: **Investment Pays**.

Now you have an overview of the process, the next section gives you more detailed prompts and tips to help smooth you on your way.

# The Tale of Two Bosses—Part Three: A Plan Is Made

First Boss was finishing his third coffee and developing a caffeine twitch when Second Boss finally spoke.

'We're avoiding going back to our offices, aren't we?' said Second Boss, buzzing slightly as he took a sip of his fourth cappuccino.

First Boss nodded.

'This is nonsense,' said Second Boss. 'We're grown Executives! We can handle our EAs.'

'Of course we can,' said First Boss with little conviction. 'Go us,' he said weakly.

'Come on, First Boss,' continued Second Boss. 'What do we do when we don't understand an issue?'

First Boss made the international sign for taking a drink.

'I'm serious,' said Second Boss. 'We break it down, don't we?'

'Yes,' said First Boss, slowly.

'We think about what we want to get out of something and how we're going to get it.'

'Yes,' said First Boss, warming.

'So, how about this,' said Second Boss. 'Instead of your EA holding your coat this afternoon, why don't you meet with her and ask her about her skills and what she can do for you.'

'Yes!' said First Boss. 'And instead of you reading out of the Screw-Fix catalogue all afternoon, why don't you meet with your EA and ask her about her skills and what she can do for you!'

'By Jove,' said the Second Boss. 'I think we've got it!'

Meanwhile, back on the other side of Kingdom, the two EAs were beginning to hit on ways forward too.

'I think we agree,' said First EA. 'At the moment, it's not much of a job, then?'

'No,' said Second EA. 'Not much of a job at all.'

'But we can do something about it, can't we?'

'We can?' said Second EA, picking at a callous on her index finger.

'Of course we can,' said First EA. 'We just need to talk to our new Bosses. Tell them how this is going to work.'

'Oh, I don't know...' started Second EA.

'Don't be ridiculous,' said First EA.

'It's just...' said Second EA. 'He's the Boss, isn't he? He knows what he's doing.'

First EA laughed and shook her head. 'That's your first mistake,' she said. 'Bosses know nothing. They have to be told what they do. Everyone knows that!'

Second EA's eyes opened wide. 'But Bosses tell us what to do,' she said. 'I don't think I would feel comfortable telling my Boss how it is going to work. If he wants me to take dictation all morning, he must have a reason.'

'What possible reason could he have for wanting you to take dictation for that long?'

Second EA shrugged. 'He's the Boss,' she said weakly and looked away.

'You need to grow a backbone,' said First EA. 'I'm not going to have someone who doesn't know what they're doing tell me how this is going to work,' she said, pushing herself to her feet. 'He had the morning to try and he failed.'

'But...' started Second EA.

'No buts,' said First EA. 'This Boss is going to do things my way or not at all,' she said, dusting her skirt down and running a hand through her hair. 'He had his chance. Now it's mine.'

'Are you sure...?'

'Second EA,' said First EA. 'You get nothing by being submissive.'

'I suppose you're right,' said Second EA.

'It is time to go Parental on his ass.' And with that, First EA swept from the coat cupboard, stepping on Second EA's toe as she passed.

Second EA watched her stride towards her desk and her stomach sank as she saw Second Boss walking with First Boss towards his office.

'Please,' whispered Second EA. 'Don't let it be more dictation.' She scuttled from the cupboard, sliding back into her seat just as Second Boss came alongside her.

'Hello,' he said awkwardly.

'Hello,' she said avoiding eye contact.

'Got a moment?' he asked in a strained voice.

Second EA nodded, mutely, picked up her notebook and followed him into his office.

# Planning

## The Kick-Off Meeting

The Kick-Off meeting lets Your EA know that you're starting this process *with her*. Try not to alarm her at this point. You don't want her walking away thinking you view her as incompetent or that she's about to be replaced by a better model. You need Your EA's Buy-In to get the EA you want.

At this meeting, outline what you'll be looking at and ask her to do the same:

Consider:

- The boundaries of the EA role

- The responsibilities of the role

- The expectations of the role

Your thoughts in response to these points are what you'll be discussing at the Developing part of the process.

### Kick-Off Meeting Tips

- Identify the reason for starting this process: to make your EA a fully integrated member of your team with her own responsibilities and authority

- Explain that you will be running the process, but it's a team effort between the two of you

- Ask your EA to write a list of what she does in her day-to-day role and send it to you before the *Wipe The Slate Clean Meeting*. Ask her to ignore what her job description says she does and to focus on the reality. Ask her to break down into percentages the amount of time she spends on each task

- Ask Your EA to write some thoughts down in response to the following:

  o How she views her role: what her objectives, priorities, boundaries and limits of authority are

  o How her role fits in with yours

  o How her role fits in with the organisation

  o What her goals are

- Make sure Your EA knows that she needs to be honest in her responses. Make sure she knows she's not going to get fired for saying she spends more time on one thing than she does on another—unless one thing is internet shopping and the other is her job

- Set the time for the *Wipe The Slate Clean Meeting*

- Keep this meeting short and sweet—don't get into things too deeply, that's what the *Wipe The Slate Clean Meeting* is for

## Collecting Your Thoughts

Now Your EA's busy thinking things over, you can do the same.

Just like you asked Your EA, think about:

- The boundaries of Your EA's role

- The responsibilities of the role

- The expectations of the role

It goes without saying that Your EA is an important person in your working life. But how does the EA role fit in with yours? How does it fit into the organisation?

Think about your workload. It's a given that you're superbusy: un-superbusy people don't tend to have EAs, unless they're super-rich and buy themselves one as a treat.

Review your To Do List to highlight areas which you can allocate to the EA role, such as organising the appraisals, competitor research or managing a particular budget.

If you figure out what her role is and where it sits with you and your organisation, it will make stage two easier. With this in mind, it's best that you do a lot of your thinking after you've heard what she thinks.

## Defining Your EA

### The Job Description

Once you have Your EA's initial thoughts, get hold of her Job Description and look at the two documents alongside one another.

Ask yourself the questions:

- Does this job description accurately reflect the responsibilities of the role?

- Does it demonstrate the authority she holds?

- Are her core objectives clear?

- Are her priorities, boundaries and authority appropriate?

Think about those comfortable ways of working that you've both slipped into that get the job done but, in reality, just don't meet either of your needs. For example:

- Did you used to have daily catch-ups but now you seem to only do them as you dash past to a meeting?

- Did Your EA used to give you a print out of your diary for the next day each evening but this has dribbled off to when you remember to ask?

- Did you used to buy your EA an almond croissant on the way into work on Friday mornings?

Now, you're both uninformed and out of the loop, and your EA is pointedly staring at you when you come in each week empty handed.

## When Boundaries And Priorities Go Wild

One of the EAs I coached had an interesting revelation with her Boss when they went through this process together.

Both the EA and her Boss knew that there was a post-script to the EA's job description. This post-script went something like this:

'To assist the Sales Team on an *ad hoc* basis, as and when necessary'

What became clear to both the EA and the Boss, however, was that what her Boss perceived of as being 'as and when necessary' was very different to what the EA was experiencing.

While her Boss expected his EA to be working with the Sales Team on a limited basis, his EA was finding herself regularly caught up with supporting them.

The main problem was this:

The Boss presented the Sales Report each week at the Exec meeting. Part of the EA's job was to support her Boss as he prepared the Sales Report by collating the various sub-reports from the Sales Team. What the Boss did not realise was that this meant his EA was spending around eight hours a week chasing, helping and, in some cases, preparing the copy for the Sales Team sub-reports to ensure they submitted their elements on time.

As far as she was concerned, the EA was following her job description and was performing as requested by her Boss.

But as they worked through this process together, the Boss was shocked to see that his EA had listed 'supporting the Sales Team' as 35 percent of her job. Together they realised that not only did the Boss not realise the extent of support the EA was giving to the Sales Team, but that the EA did not realise that she shouldn't be giving this level of support either, despite it being on her agreed job description.

How did this happen? This happened because of the dreaded term '*Ad hoc*'.

**The Perils Of The Dreaded *Ad Hoc***

*Ad hoc* is the catch-all that gets added to most Job Descriptions. You may have one on yours, too. It's the one that goes: 'To provide support to the department as a whole on an *ad hoc* basis'.

*Ad hoc* is dangerous for two reasons:

- It removes boundaries

- It removes core priorities

In fact, I would like to remove *ad hoc* from business-speak altogether. For a start, it has two *very* different meanings:

- A solution for a specific task

- Makeshift or improvised

When used in job descriptions, I firmly believe it is most likely referring to the second. It is easier to ask someone to 'improvise' their support to the department than to restrict them to a definition.

The result is that if your EA sees someone struggling with something in the team and no-one can help, she feels duty-bound to step in. This is why the EA mentioned above was essentially preparing the Sales Team's report for them. This is why Your EA may be minuting a meeting that you're not in. Or why she's scanning a document that has nothing to do with you. Or why you bumped into Your EA last night sweating over the comb-binder at seven o'clock.

*Ad hoc* results in the regular cry of 'I don't suppose you'd be able to help me label these files/add some graphs to this report/chase me for that content?'

It encourages a buddy-buddy situation: 'I know you're not my EA, but you'll do this for me, won't you?'

Or a manipulative one: 'I know Your Boss wants this, but I'm so busy. If you help me, I'll get it to your Boss on time'.

And because Your EA is conscientious and wants to do her best for you and the company, she does it.

Plus, it's on her job description.

Get a big, black marker pen and scrub out the term *ad hoc*.

In fact, get a big, black marker pen and scrub out the phrase 'Support the whole Department, where necessary'.

### How To Get Rid Of *Ad Hoc*

If you're happy for Your EA to provide support to the Sales Team, insert some boundaries. Either agree with the Team and Your EA specific tasks and time allowances for her to support the Sales Team, or ask HR to do this. If the team already have an assistant who's just not quite up to speed yet, insist the assistant is their first point of call and remove Your EA from their grasp.

At the very least, Your EA should know what is *expected* of her from *everyone*. Give her permission to push back.

And, once this is agreed you must *communicate* this to all the relevant people. (See Section 2—Managing the Relationship.)

### The Importance Of Boundaries

By following the actions described above, you are implementing boundaries for Your EA.

Boundaries are key to ensuring Your EA's energy and focus is in the right direction: Yours.

As an example, when you're on a plane, if you need oxygen, you're told to put your mask on first before you help anyone else. You can't help anyone if you're flailing around trying to breathe.

Clear boundaries are Your EA's metaphorical oxygen mask: she looks after what she's supposed to do and once that's done, she can do the other, clearly defined elements of her job description. It limits any frustrated flailing.

Ultimately clarity on boundaries creates structure.

And through structure comes value.

## Priorities

Boundaries also help people understand priorities—Your priorities, Your EA's priorities and Your Department's priorities.

### Establishing Priorities

First look at the current job description and compare it to what Your EA has listed or told you she does. Identify those areas that are new to you or that you're not happy with, such as the amount of time she's spending with the Sales Team.

Now you know what she's doing, you have an understanding of how she sees the role.

From this, consider: what are her priorities?

Think about what *you* want to be Your EA's priorities. It may be a very simple answer: *Me*.

Which is perfectly acceptable. Most bosses want their EA's priorities to be them. Why shouldn't you be their priority?

So, if we all agree that her first priority is you, let's have that as Number One:

*Me* (her boss)

But does that feel too general? How about:

*Supporting my needs and deadlines.*

Too general again?

How can you define her priorities to ensure her boundaries are clear?

By analysing your own workload.

## Your Workload Is Your EA's Workload?

I once coached a top-level EA who described herself as 'the highest paid tea-lady in London'. Why? Because her boss did all the work while she made all the tea. I will come back to this in more detail later when we're talking about Managing the Relationship, but for now let's look at this from a Managing the Role angle.

*What does having an EA who feels like a Tea-Lady say about her Boss?*

Consider Your EA. Consider her role as we have been doing above and think about how she supports your workload delivery.

Look at your priorities.

• What are your priorities?

- What are Your EA's priorities?

- Do your priorities and hers ever meet?

  o If they do, is it working?

  o If they don't, how would they look if they did?

By establishing her Priorities in conjunction with your own workload you are moving into a whole other sphere of Boss/EA working. She is truly becoming your Business Partner.

But there's one last thing that you should consider before you plunge in: Your EA's goals.

## Your EA's Goals

This won't surprise you at all, seeing as you are well immersed in this process now and are truly in touch with your inner-EA, but EAs are like Bosses: they have their own professional and personal goals.

It goes without saying that it is your EA's responsibility to ensure that her professional goals are achieved, but the sign of a good boss is one who takes responsibility for helping her get there.

Consider this: many EAs have university degrees or diplomas in subjects related to your industry. They may have practical skills like graphic design or writing that they would love to bring into their job. If there is scope in the role, why not investigate how their skills and knowledge can be used for the benefit of the company, you and for Your EA.

And don't worry if your EA's goals seem to outstretch how you'd seen the role; maybe she'll give you ideas for the future.

## What Type Of EA Do You Want?

This is probably one of the most important things to consider, and it often gets forgotten.

While boundaries, priorities and goals are key, you should also be thinking about the type of EA you have. What are Your EA's strengths? What does she do particularly well? Is she great with clients or does she really understand the chemistry of your department?

For example: lots of EAs are considered to be the lynchpins of offices and departments. They know what's going on and can usually sense trouble looming before it appears. Is this the sort of EA that you have?

Other EAs are seen as fantastic diplomats and can be sent in before or after feathers have been ruffled.

Make the most of what you have.

# Developing

Now you've had time to think about what Your EA is doing now and what Your EA will be doing going forward, you should have some excellent notes and plans for the *Wipe The Slate Clean Meeting.*

## Planning The Meeting

You know what you want to talk about, now quickly consider the following as you set up the meeting:

- *Where shall we meet?* If you work in an open plan office, would a meeting room work, or is that too formal? Would your office be too distracting? Would a cafe be too informal? The Ivy too flash? Between the two of you decide on a mutually acceptable place.

- *What time shall we meet?* Are you both morning people? Or do you peak at lunchtime? What about Your EA? When is she at her most productive? Make your meeting for the best time for both of you.

- Ensure that you have your plan clearly drawn up for the meeting.

- Identify in your plan who is responsible for what by when. If you want to make things happen you have to drive them.

## The *Wipe The Slate Clean Meeting*

It would be tempting to walk into this meeting as though walking into a job interview, what with all the changes that are going to need to be discussed. But if you're feeling in the slightest bit apprehensive, don't be! This is a positive thing. This is about re-establishing a way of working together that is effective, productive and enjoyable.

You've done all the groundwork, now it's time to challenge yourselves to do things differently.

So before you even go in, let's quickly address something which may help with the decision making.

### Communication

The most important thing for you to bear in mind when considering communicating with your EA is this:

**Your EA is your Business Partner and, as such, she is your equal. Your communication style with your EA should reflect that.**

When we talk to someone, what we're saying is only a fraction of what we're actually communicating. The trick is this: what you say is only 7 percent of how you communicate (verbal). How you say it (vocal) makes up 38 percent—this is the tone of voice that you use—and how you look (the body language) when you're saying it is a whopping 55 percent.

Bear this in mind when you're talking with your EA. It is important that you make Your EA feel at ease during this meeting for two important reasons:

1. It's very common for an EA to be filled with a sense of dread if she needs to interrupt her boss.

2. It's also very common for an EA to be intimidated by her boss in a professional capacity.

You want Your EA to feel comfortable and confident enough to communicate with you as your Business Partner.

This leads us to something you may have already come across:

### Eric Berne's Transactional Analysis—Parent/Adult/Child

Eric Berne identified three alter-ego states that people slip into in different situations. He talked about moderating and influencing your communication to get the best out of people around you by utilising these states:

**Parent**—an aggressive state which displays non-compromising attitudes, tells people what to do. There is no negotiation in this state.

**Adult**—an assertive position with own views and opinions whilst hearing others. The adult seeks to find a middle ground which works for all.

**Child**—the passive or submissive state, wanting to put ideas forward but not having confidence or permission to do so.

Berne says that we are capable of slipping in and out of each aspect depending on our environment, but we all have a dominant style.

While the optimum state is Adult/Assertive, you will find that many EAs, while interacting with their bosses, perform within the Child/Submissive position. Of course, Your EA may not, in which case you may find yourself in the Child position with a

Parental EA. But for the majority, we should consider the former as the standard.

Your EA may well be in the Child/Submissive state when operating around senior executives. There is an historical reason for this: women have traditionally worked for men. In the past they have received less formal education and worked in what has previously been seen as a non-essential business role. Equally, having a manager who displays Parent/Aggressive tendencies can push people into Child/Submissive, even those who are Adult/Assertive in other situations.

One of the key phrases from this previous paragraph is '**non-essential business role**'. If Your EA perceives her role to be such, then she will naturally feel submissive to your 'essential business role'.

Be aware of that. Not only is it not true, but it is damaging. It most certainly should not be left as the 'norm'. Submissive equals reactive, and this limits Your EA and her effectiveness.

It is vital that you interact in, and encourage, the Adult/Assertive position with Your EA in all your communication (this will be discussed further in Section Two), but you should also be aware that it will be, at first, an unnatural and uncomfortable state for your EA to be in. For women, assertiveness can often be perceived as aggression. Your EA needs to be able to exercise her assertiveness and to understand the difference.

For this meeting, and moving forward, make sure Your EA understands that she has your permission to be assertive.

**Content**

You've already done your homework so you know exactly what you're discussing. But bear in mind that Your EA has been doing the same.

To keep things to the point and clear draw up your list before the meeting and email it to Your EA. Use this as an agenda.

Be mindful that you don't dominate or become Parental during the meeting. This is a meeting for you both to discuss how Your EA can provide more meaningful and appropriate support to you. Stay focused on this.

Above all, you both need to come to the meeting with open minds and flexible attitudes.

**Flexibility—You and Your EA**

You've both had plenty of time to get excited and enthused about the plans you have for the role since the Kick-Off meeting.

But you should be aware that you've not talked about these plans with each other yet.

Your EA has to be as flexible as you in this new approach, and the two of you need to accept that you will both have ideas. She may want to do something you hadn't considered. Be flexible. You may want her to do something she hadn't considered. She should be flexible too. If you're not sure what you think about one of her suggestions, take it away with you to think about and encourage her to do the same with yours. Neither of you, whatever you do, should dismiss a suggestion out of hand. Unless it's deeply inappropriate or illegal.

Remind Your EA that you and she may hear things you either don't like or you don't want to hear. How you respond to these will make all the difference going forward.

**Outcome**

Your EA should come out of the meeting understanding:

- Her role as Your EA, including expectations and objectives

- How she fits in with your role

- How she fits in with the organisation

- Believing that you understand her goals

You should come out of the meeting understanding:

- Your EA's role, including expectations and objectives

- How she fits in with your role

- How she fits in with the organisation

- What Your EA's goals are

Together you should come out of the meeting with a clear strategy for working together for self, team and defined outcomes. That strategy should include timed actions for you and Your EA to achieve the newly defined role.

# The Tale of Two Bosses—Part Four: How First Boss Got What He Wanted

'Excuse me First Boss,' said First EA appearing at the door to his office, notepad in hand and a stern look on her face.

First Boss jumped. 'Yes!' he said a little too loudly. 'Yes,' he repeated. 'Come in, First EA. It is always a pleasure.' He rounded his desk, and patted on the chair that sat on the opposite side to his own.

First EA looked sternly at him again and sat.

'Thank you,' she said, smoothing down her skirt and opening her notebook firmly.

First Boss found his own chair and sat down, steadying himself as it began to turn beneath his weight.

'I'm glad you're here. I wanted to apologise about...' he began.

'This morning was unacceptable,' interrupted First EA, her eyes cool.

'I...' said First Boss in surprise. 'Well, yes,' he said. 'I was about to...'

'I want you to know that that is the first and only time you will be treating me like that,' continued

First EA. 'You should know that I am an EA of eight years standing. I have a diploma in project management and I have managed secretarial teams,' she said. 'If you don't know this, I take it as an insult—what Boss worth his salt doesn't know his EA's CV?'

Boss shook his head ferociously and made a noise of agreement, sounding a little like a cow.

'Good,' said First EA. 'Because we need to start as we mean to go on, don't we Boss,' she said.

First Boss nodded enthusiastically again and wiped his sweating palms on the front of his trousers.

'So,' she said. 'I have drawn up a plan for us so there are no arguments going forward.' She stopped and leant forward, keeping her steely eye upon First Boss. 'I don't like arguments,' she said.

First Boss gulped.

'We shall meet first thing every day,' she said, using her pen to point to each line she had written in her notebook. 'I shall manage your diary. If you wish to put anything in, it must go through me. Any deviation will result in you losing a privilege for the week. Three deviations will result in you being grounded from any lunch meetings which do not take place in the lunchroom here.' She looked up. 'For a month.' She ducked her head towards him. 'Do I make myself clear?'

First Boss nodded meekly as the blood began to drain from his cheeks.

And so the list went on, each instruction firmer than the last until finally she stopped, closed her notebook and sat back.

'Now then,' said First EA. 'I imagine you have a few questions.'

First Boss opened his mouth.

'Keep them short and to the point,' said First EA. 'I can't bear bores.'

First Boss took a deep breath and his hands gripped the armrests of his chair. Feel the force, said a voice from inside his head. Feel the force of the Adult. And he felt a smile blossom for the first time since First EA had strode into his office and all of a sudden he felt the strength of who he was inside and he was filled with the joy of being First Boss again.

'First EA,' he said, leaning forward. 'I like a lot of your plans,' he said. 'I really do.'

First EA stared coldly back. An eyebrow twitched.

'I think this will absolutely work,' said First Boss.

'Good,' said First EA. 'You just have to do what I say and it will.'

'With all due respect First EA,' said First Boss, his heart in his mouth but the knowledge of truth in his heart. 'I think that the way this is going to work is if we are a team, together.'

'A team needs a leader,' interrupted First EA.

'Indeed,' said First Boss. 'But how does this sound? You lead in your role, and I lead in mine. And when we work together, we work...together.'

'But...' said First EA, two small circles of red on her cheeks deepening to rose.

'You are clearly a great EA. I know you are because the King hired you. But this isn't going to work if you just boss me about,' said First Boss, eyes shining as the words flew from him.

'But...' said First EA. 'I am your EA,' she said. 'I must boss you about.'

'Well you can,' said First Boss. 'But you will really tire yourself out.'

First EA's mouth flapped a little.

'Look,' said First Boss. 'I know it is difficult when you first start working with people and I have never had an EA before. But I like the idea of us working together. You clearly know what you're doing,' he said and First EA flushed even more. 'And I will need you to direct me in the best way for me to use you. I need your knowledge.'

A smile suddenly appeared on First EA's face. 'You do,' she said warmly.

'And you need my support,' First Boss said.

The smile deepened. 'I do,' First EA said.

'So, let us look at your list again,' First Boss said.

'And let us talk through each point together,' said First EA.

'And once we have agreed how we are going to work together, I will let the Kingdom know what your role is so that there are no conflicts or problems. I will let them know how you fit into the Kingdom and also with them.'

'Everyone will know what my boundaries are and what your expectations are,' agreed First EA.

'Perfect,' said First Boss.

'Perfect,' said First EA.

At last, the First EA did not feel the need to run First Boss like he was a child, and First Boss did not feel the need to take out a contract on the First EA at the earliest opportunity. It was, as they say, the start of a beautiful business partnership.

# Implementing

## Communicating And Committing

The hard work doesn't stop yet.

It is important that during this transition into the new way of working that you protect and communicate Your EA's priorities. At the top of your list of *Things To Do* should now be to communicate Your EA's responsibilities to your colleagues.

You may have removed a lot of the Sales Team support from Your EA's role, but they won't know this unless you tell them. And, be aware, that if Your EA tries to tell them, it could cause problems. Your EA could always draft this missive for you, but make sure it goes out as soon as possible to avoid any awkwardness between Your EA and the team. Communicate to the team that there has been a shift in how the two of you are working together going forwards, and outline her newly defined authority and the core business focus of her role.

## Stick To The Process

It is equally important that the commitment you showed in setting up the meeting is continued as soon as you walk away. If you have agreed to sign Your EA up for project management training and it's your action to confirm this with HR, make sure that you do it.

Wavering on either side will cause a change in working relationship—an element of mistrust may slip in, or disillusionment.

# Reviewing

## The Check-In Meeting

Set the time for the Check-In Meeting during the *Wipe The Slate Clean Meeting* so you can see it approaching. Keep a note of the things that are working from your meeting and things that aren't. Come to the meeting with the same open-minded flexibility in your Adult/Assertive mode ready to remedy and reinforce the process.

It's okay to say that something you suggested isn't working. It's also okay to say that something Your EA suggested isn't working either. Maybe you don't actually need your calendar printed each evening after all.

Equally, it's okay to say when something *is* working and grow from that. Your EA may have more time freed up from no longer supporting the Sales Team so extensively and has had time to think more about the research project you'd discussed during the Directors' Meeting. Now that you've given her more authority, she feels confident enough to take elements of this on.

## Accept It Takes Time

Remember: this is a process. It's not set in stone. What you decide at the *Wipe The Slate Clean Meeting* is just the beginning: your working life together is what's important. Don't be afraid to highlight areas that need work or you can do without help. Keep the process moving, growing, evolving and, above all, keep communicating.

## In Brief

This section has given you the steps necessary to Managing the Role of Your EA effectively. You have explored the process of defining, understanding and meet *your* expectations of the role of Your EA.

You have done this by implementing the Investment Process: Managing The Role, which covers four simple steps:

- **Planning**

  Thinking about Your EA's role and how it's working for you. Planning what you would like the role to be and considering its boundaries and priorities.

- **Developing**

  Working together with Your EA to prepare new working practices to improve the existing processes

- **Implementing**

  Putting into practice the plans you and Your EA have made.

- **Reviewing**

  To continually review together how things are working and make changes where necessary.

I have shown you the value of boundaries and priorities in the role of Your EA, and how having these in place will ensure that Your EA's role meets all expectations.

The way you do it comes down to your Working Relationship. This is an area which is just as important as Your EA's Role and as we move into Section Two, we will look at how you and Your EA work together and how this can be improved to work in conjunction with this Investment Process.

So, let's move onto the second strand of working effectively with Your EA: Managing the Relationship.

# The Tale of Two Bosses—Part Five: How Second Boss Did Not Get What He Wanted

Second Boss leant forward in his chair and patted Second EA's hand.

'It's okay,' said Second Boss. 'You haven't done anything wrong.'

Second EA shook her head and sniffed.

Second Boss sat back and looked around anxiously. 'Is there anything I can do?' he asked.

Second EA shook her head and sniffed again.

'Maybe we should come back to this when you're feeling a bit more...'

'Yes,' squeaked Second EA.

'Because I really did not mean to make you cry,' said Second Boss. 'I just wanted to discuss how you saw the role. I wasn't criticising you.'

'No,' squeaked Second EA.

'It makes it hard for me to have a conversation with you when you're crying, though.'

'I'm not crying,' squeaked Second EA.

'Okay,' said Second Boss.

The sound of Second EA trying not to cry filled the office.

'Right,' said Second Boss. 'I'm going to get some water,' he said. 'Why don't I get you something and then when I come back we'll carry on where we left off.'

'Okay,' said Second EA.

A few moments later, Second Boss returned and Second EA, although puffy eyed and slightly damp around the nose, seemed to be somewhat more composed.

'Are you feeling better?' asked Second Boss, cautiously handing over the glass of water.

Second EA nodded and gratefully took a sip.

'Good,' said Second Boss. 'So, I wanted to discuss how you thought this role would work. How you thought you fitted into the company. What you thought you could bring to working for me.'

Second EA's chin wobbled. 'Yes,' she said.

'Yes to...' said Second Boss.

'Yes,' whispered Second EA. 'I could bring a lot to working for you.'

'Good,' said Second Boss, relieved that she had not started crying again. 'Any ideas of something specific?'

Second EA shrugged and sat for a moment.

'Let's talk about what I want then,' said Second Boss. 'And maybe that will prompt you.'

'Okay,' whispered Second EA.

'Well,' said Second Boss. 'I'm fine with my emails and my correspondence, but where I struggle is with tender submissions.'

Second EA nodded, twisting the tissue in her hands. 'I sort of know how to do those,' she said. 'If you tell me what to do.'

'Good,' said Second Boss. 'Sometimes I forget to put things in the diary.'

'Oh,' said Second EA. 'Can you try and remember?'

Second Boss shrugged. 'I suppose...'

'Because I find it easier to do what I am told as an EA.'

'Oh,' said Second Boss.

'That way,' said Second EA. 'You know what you are getting and I know what you want from me.'

Something out of the corner of Second Boss's eye distracted him. He could see First Boss and his EA shaking hands in his office. Shaking hands and smiling at one another. He wondered if they were shaking hands over First Boss agreeing to tell First EA how to do her job.

'I don't mean to speak out of turn,' interrupted Second EA softly. 'I would just rather not make a mistake. It's better that you tell me what to do and I do it.'

'That's fine,' said Second Boss.

He sighed and Second EA sniffed.

'Let's just see how it goes.'

Second Boss attempted to smile encouragingly at Second EA who began to cry again as she left the office.

Second Boss stared at his Outlook without seeing it. He was worrying. He was worrying about what to do with his EA. He did not want to make her cry but he wasn't sure how he could avoid it if he were to have the EA he wanted.

As he worried he decided not to look in the direction of First Boss and his EA for a while. It was too upsetting seeing how well they were working together.

Second Boss was beginning to get the impression that maybe Second EA was not the right EA for him after all.

# Section 2: Managing the Relationship

As I explained earlier, there are two strands to a great working relationship:

- Managing the Role

- Managing the Relationship

You have already established *what* Your EA does, but for it to actually succeed, you also need to manage the relationship. Of course, in the real world, you work on these two strands alongside one another at the same time, but for simplicity's sake I have separated them.

Section Two looks at Managing the Relationship to ensure that you work together effectively, efficiently and, most importantly, successfully.

## The Boss/EA Relationship

Your EA is someone you enjoy working with, trust implicitly and who can always be relied upon to provide quality support. In return, you are a trustworthy boss who is open and honest with Your EA and communicates appropriately with her ensuring she knows what your priorities are.

In an ideal world.

Throw in a couple of personalities, demanding lifestyles and pressing deadlines and perhaps some of those things stop being quite so important. I mean, she has access to your diary so is it essential to tell her every little thing you're doing? And she always insists on coming in when you've finally got a few minutes to yourself. You like her and all, but you don't need to talk to her *all the time*, do you?

Now we're probably somewhere closer to where you are with Your EA at the moment. And it's working okay.

Still, there's always room for improvement.

This section identifies why having a good working relationship with Your EA can change your working life. While you may already have Your EA's new priorities and boundaries in mind, it is vital that you continue to consider these alongside Managing The Relationship, to ensure that fantastic opportunities for improvement aren't lost in misunderstanding, frustration or, even worse, apathy.

With all the energy you're putting into this, having an EA you enjoy working with is surely the cherry on top?

## The Investment Part Two: The Relationship

An excellent working relationship will create excellent results. You know that. Think of your colleagues and your interactions with the ones you work well with and the ones you don't. Which do you think of when you're pulling a project team together? Probably not the one you overheard moaning about you at last Friday night's drinks. Or the one who put red pen all the way through your report instead of discussing it with you.

Your relationship with Your EA is the same; she is your Business Partner after all.

You may not socialise together (and often that's for the best—knowing what happens to your EA when she drinks tequila isn't necessarily going to add anything to your mutual productivity) and she may enjoy hardcore techno when she's not sitting at your desk, while you prefer improvised jazz. These things don't matter. What matters is how you work together.

The Investment Process: The Relationship works in conjunction with the Investment Process: The Role and follows the following three stages:

- Identify

- Improve

- Review

**Note**

These steps appear simpler than the **Investment Process: The Role**, but as they are more emotional than practical in their focus, they can be harder to change.

This is why it is important that while you are considering these stages you ensure that you use established business practices such as appraisals, reviews and catch-ups so that you can discuss any agreed changes that are necessary or have already been implemented in a professional and safe forum.

## 1. Identify

To understand how to work together effectively, you need to identify how you work now and how you want to work going forward.

This stage of the process looks specifically at:

- What a Relationship is

- What Communication is

- What your Working Relationship style is

At the end of this process you should know where you are and have an understanding of what you need to do in the next step to improve.

## 2. Improve

Understanding how you communicate and how your relationship with Your EA is working should help you identify areas where you want to improve.

In particular, during this stage of the process you will examine the business practices that, when applied appropriately, support the development and improvement of working relationships. With this in mind, this stage focuses on Appraisals and Acknowledgements.

## 3. Review

As with any process, to ensure the transition is successful it must be reviewed as it's applied to ensure it fits with who you both are and what you both want.

# The Four Tenets of an Amazing (Working) Relationship

Your relationship with your EA is a lot like every other relationship in your life. It consists of four basic tenets:

- **Trust**—it takes a while to trust someone, but you have to be able to trust Your EA as soon as possible. If you don't, it will show.

- **Respect**—if you treat your EA with anything other than respect, Your EA will respond accordingly.

- **Honest Communication**—don't lie to Your EA or about Your EA. If you missed a deadline because you missed it, don't blame your EA in a meeting. Or if you missed a deadline because Your EA missed it, let her know. The only time you're allowed to lie is if it's her birthday and that is a cake in your bag.

- **Love**—don't cuddle your EA, but do treat her like she's a person with feelings.

As in any relationship, if one of these slips, an imbalance occurs. Of course, spending your whole time focusing on whether your EA feels trusted, respected, not-lied-to and loved will send you crazy and, more than likely, get you fired and/or a restraining order, but if you just bear them in mind, you should be fine.

So that's the fluffy stuff.

How do you apply these tenets in the cold hard light of day when there's an EA out there you don't know how to approach and the last time you asked her to do something she cried?

## What Communication Is

We briefly touched on Communication in Section One.

We discussed Eric Berne's Parent/Adult/Child model and stressed the importance of you and Your EA both adopting the Adult-Assertive position.

We also discussed how the most important thing for you to bear in mind when communicating with Your EA is that Your EA is your Business Partner and, as such, she is your equal.

Let's come back to this now in more detail: communicating with Your EA as your Business Partner.

How did you talk to your EA this morning when you first came in? Did you speak to her in the same way you would speak to a colleague? To a senior? To the COO?

Of course, there may be an element of familiarity and jocularity between you depending on your relationship, but I'm hoping you didn't ignore her, or mumble 'hello' as you rushed past or lay across her desk weeping because your rugby team lost last night.

As I explained in Section One, when we talk to someone, what we're saying is only a fraction of what we're actually communicating. What you say is only 7 percent of how you communicate (verbal). How you say it (vocal) makes up 38 percent, and how you look (visual) when you're saying it is 55 percent.

So how are you communicating with your EA right now?

Are you conveying the right message? When you were late for a meeting because your EA had put it into the diary at the wrong time, did you react aggressively or passively? Did you communicate your annoyance professionally—i.e. with visual, verbal and vocal tones bases covered—or did you use your body language and tone of voice to convey your anger?

## Miscommunication—A Common Mixup

Let's imagine that the first thing you said when you saw Your EA this morning was:

'Lisa, can you make sure the Exec meeting actually starts at eleven today? Last time it started at ten-thirty and Bob wasn't impressed.'

As far as you were concerned, you were simply asking her to check the time of the meeting because the Director's EA had forgotten to let Your EA know the last-minute time-change of the previous meeting.

This morning, however, you're annoyed about something completely different.

Your train was delayed which means you won't be able to get to the barbers at lunchtime and your hair will look crap at the drinks tonight which are important because the new CFO will be there and your wife made a comment about you looking like a hippy this morning.

This annoyance is in your voice as you speak to Lisa and while you're not annoyed with her you're too annoyed with everything else to care.

So what Lisa hears is a criticism. Lisa knows full well that it was a miscommunication from the Director's office which led to you being late rather than Lisa making a mistake in the diary. But when she gently reminds you, you snap that it's not important. Because you too know that it wasn't Lisa's fault but you're not going over *that* again, not when you're already thirty minutes late starting the day.

Now two people's backs are up: yours for having a bad-hair-day, Lisa's for being unfairly growled at for something that was out of her control.

The meaning that Lisa takes from your passing comment is not what you intended.

While Lisa equally needs to ensure she doesn't take things personally, if *all* requests are communicated to her in that careless way, she'll gradually begin to either lose confidence or grow resentful.

Of course, no-one's expecting you to consider every single little word and action when you're communicating with your EA. That's a one-way ticket to lunacy. But it isn't unreasonable for you to be more aware of how you come across to ensure that you are communicating appropriately. Indeed, once you've got the hang of this with your EA, you may end up having to say a whole lot less than you ever did before you started this process.

## Communicating With Confidence

Ensuring that you communicate appropriately means that Your EA will be comfortable approaching you. Which is the whole point! Having a confident EA is multiplying her effectiveness for you a hundred fold.

When an EA is confident with you, she will use her initiative and initiative is the EA's secret weapon. She will feel able to tell you when she thinks there's a problem in your diary; she'll be able to divert emails knowing you won't bring down the Wrath of Boss on her. She'll spot something in the Exec minutes that she knows she can do for you more quickly than you could ask her. She'll push for you to meet even when you say you're busy so that you can go through your diary and she'll boldly knock on doors when something is vital to ensure you are passed urgent priorities.

Your confident EA will not be the one scurrying around the meeting room table, nervously passing you a message wishing the world would swallow her up while all the other Big Cheeses acknowledge her inferiority. Your confident EA won't let you miss a diary meeting because you're a bit busy, she'll either make it snappy or she'll fit herself in as soon as possible.

Your confident EA will be your partner in success.

## Your Working Relationship Style

You may recall in Section One I referred to a client I had coached. She was a top EA in the City, looking after an enormously Big Cheese. When we first met, however, she was very low and felt completely helpless. Indeed, she told me that she felt like 'the highest paid tea-lady in London'.

Now, while making teas and coffees is often part of an EA's working life, it was clear that, for someone of this EA's experience and quality to be feeling that disconnected with the rest of her role, and her Boss, there was a certain imbalance.

Her Boss had replaced the previous Big Cheese with whom this EA had had a fantastic, intuitive working relationship. The new Boss had come into his new role not really knowing what his new EA did. Because this Boss was not as clued-up as you, dear reader, he had not applied the Investment Process to his new working relationship and, as such, had simply come to rely on giving out orders as and when he needed anything, remaining locked away for the rest of the time. The only thing that appeared to be established at this point was a Parent/Child working relationship.

A few years later and the new Boss had a superior EA who was ready to leave because she was bored to tears and deeply unchallenged.

You'd think, then, that the EA had a terrible relationship with her Boss but, as we chatted, I discovered that the EA actually really quite liked her Boss. Indeed, she felt they got on well. Which is why she was so disappointed that she was so unhappy in the role.

So what was the problem? Why did she feel so lousy about her job and why didn't he feel that he could trust her with a proper EA role?

Essentially their relationship was completely out of whack.

## Bruce Tuckman's Stages of Group Development

You may have heard of Bruce Tuckman and his Stages of Group Development. Tuckman proposed this system in 1965 as a way to understand the stages that groups go through in order to work together to achieve success.

These were developed in relation to larger groups. That said, you and Your EA are still a group—just a small one.

The four stages that Tuckman suggested were:

1. **Forming:** trying to get things right with the unfamiliar.

2. **Storming:** the honeymoon period is over; moving towards a partnership with some periods of jostling as things settle down.

3. **Norming:** roles are settled and you are working together

4. **Performing:** purposeful, operating strategically together for self, team and defined outcomes.

The trick of the Tuckman Stages of Group Development is that the development cannot be a static 'thing'. Like a shark, you have to keep moving forward through the stages. Static, circular movement in one stage is a red flag.

With this in mind, let's see why the Highest Paid Tea-Lady in London was feeling so despondent with her likeable Boss.

When we first met, we went through the Tuckman Stages and the EA placed herself at Norming. Both she and her Boss were working together fine, maybe not how she wanted but the roles were settled and they got along well. Then, on our second meeting, she greeted me with wide-eyed excitement. She had gone away and thought about Tuckman's process and realised that she and her Boss weren't actually at Norming at all. They weren't even at Storming. After two years, the Tea-Lady EA and her Big Cheese Boss were stuck at Forming.

This revelation made everything clear: no wonder she felt it impossible to be anything but Child/Submissive and why she did not feel that things were improving, only going downhill.

Newly armed with this wisdom, the EA went back to her role with fresh eyes and within a month she proudly proclaimed that she and her Boss were happily jostling in the Storming stage. She was no longer the Child and he was no longer the Parent. They were storming together as Adults.

## How To Apply Tuckman To Your Working Relationship With Your EA

Think about your working relationship with Your EA.

- How would you describe your working relationship?

- Do you work together as a team? Is there one person who drives the relationship?

- Are you happy with your answers?

- Where do the answers you have given point to you being in Tuckman's Stages?

- How long have you been in that stage?

- How long do you think before you can move into the next stage?

Once you're clear on this, ask Your EA what her thoughts are. Ask her where she thinks you are in Tuckman's Stages. Does it match what you thought?

# The Tale of Two Bosses—Part Six: The Myth of the Psychic EA

So the two Bosses settled in to their working life with their new EAs.

Over the weeks, First Boss really started to shine. He was working well with his EA and it showed: he stopped working late and he was full of ideas at the board meeting. Every morning, First Boss and First EA would sit in his office together and run through his diary and plan his priorities. All was well for First Boss.

On the other side of the office, however, Second Boss watched First Boss with First EA and glowered beneath a dark, rumbling cloud of envy. While Second EA was not crying nearly as much, she had rung in sick a few times, his diary was a mess and the tender submissions were still drowning him. Things had not improved.

'It's not fair,' thought Second Boss. 'My EA isn't half as good as First Boss's EA. Every time I try to resolve things with her, she just agrees.'

Then one day, with a sigh, he just gave up. Maybe it wasn't as straightforward as he thought. He knew how to do his job, and he was good at it. Maybe having an EA was not just about work, it was about magic too. Maybe the King had been right when he said that they were magical beings. Maybe that's where it was going wrong for Second Boss and his EA? Maybe his EA wasn't magical enough.

'Your EA's much more psychic than mine,' said Second Boss over coffee with First Boss one sunny Monday. 'It's obvious.'

'My EA's not psychic,' said First Boss. 'We just communicate, that's all.'

'Nonsense,' said Second Boss. 'All EAs are psychic. I know that now. My EA doesn't need me to tell her when I set up a meeting. In fact she goes all weird when I do tell her. Probably because she knows already and gets upset. You know how EAs can be.' He laughed uncomfortably to cover the fact that he did not know at all and hoped that First Boss wouldn't notice.

'I'm not sure...' said First Boss but Second Boss cut him off.

'You know just as well as I that it is not about communication, it is about magic. You're just saying that to make me feel better. You know just as well as I that the reason my EA's not working properly is because she's not psychic enough. I need a new one.'

First Boss gave Second Boss a strange look. 'Have you been working long hours again?' he asked.

'Of course,' said Second Boss flashing a sharp look back. 'What do you expect with a broken EA?'

'Get some rest and then talk to her,' said First Boss.

'I knew you'd say that,' said Second Boss and he walked away. First Boss watched him sadly—sad for his friend being upset and sad that his friend hadn't figured out how to work properly with his EA.

One afternoon, the two Bosses were in a meeting with the King and the King said to them both: 'My dearest Bosses: we must have a meeting first thing tomorrow morning to discuss the future of our kingdom for I fear we have trouble ahead. If you miss this meeting, we'll have to go ahead and make a decision without you, for the decision must be made by the chimes of half-past ten in the morning. You must be here at ten o'clock on the dot.'

First Boss said: 'I'll check with my EA, but I think that should be fine.'

Second Boss, anxious to prove to the King that his EA was just as good as First Boss's, said: 'I'm sending her a message with my mind now. I shall be here tomorrow at ten o'clock.'

After the meeting, although it finished at seven o'clock in the evening and both of the EAs had already gone home, First Boss sent an email to First EA marked: 'Please Read First Thing'. It told First EA about the plan for the ten o'clock meeting and asked her to reschedule his diary to fit this meeting.

Second Boss went to a bar to meet some friends and had a very nice Pinot Noir.

The next morning dawned and First EA rearranged the meeting that First Boss had originally had for ten o'clock with his Client Director. When First Boss arrived, First EA handed him some paperwork she thought might help with the Big Important Meeting with the King. At ten minutes before ten o'clock, First EA reminded First Boss of the Big Important Meeting with the King and First Boss happily headed to the King's office with time to spare.

On the other side of the office, however, Second Boss was slightly late for a telephone conference that morning (thanks to the second bottle of Pinot Noir) and so had not had a chance to check that Second EA had received his psychic message that the Big Important Meeting with the King was happening.

Second Boss became embroiled in the telephone conference and it was not until twenty minutes after ten o'clock that Second Boss noticed the time. Slamming down the phone, Second Boss flew from the conference room and roared at Second EA:

'Why didn't you tell me what the time was?'

'I didn't realise you needed to know,' replied Second EA, and burst into tears.

'I've got the Big Important Meeting!' Second Boss shouted. 'You know, the one at ten o'clock! With the King!'

'I don't know what meeting you're talking about,' said Second EA, almost hysterical.

'I sent you my message last night!' Second Boss was turning red with fury. 'I had to be there. I'm late! I'm late!'

So Second Boss sprinted away, arriving at the King's office sweaty and out of breath. The King's EA stood at the door sadly shaking her head.

'I'm sorry,' she said. 'But the King needed you here at ten o'clock. As you were not here, you're no longer part of the decision.'

'But! But! My EA is broken!' spluttered Second Boss. 'She's not psychic at all! She didn't tell me about the meeting!'

'My dear Boss,' said the King's EA to Second Boss. 'What on earth made you think your EA was psychic?'

'Well, because...' said Second Boss. 'Because she...' Second Boss frowned. 'First Boss's EA always knows what that Boss is doing!' the Boss snapped. 'She's psychic and so should mine be.'

'Oh Second Boss,' said the EA to the King. 'First Boss's EA isn't psychic.'

'She's not?' said Second Boss, confused.

'No,' said the King's EA. 'First Boss and First EA have something else much more powerful that they use.'

'What is it?' Second Boss crouched down by the EA's desk and whispered: 'I beg of you: tell me what they have. I will give anything to know.'

The EA ducked her head so that she was level with Second Boss's face. 'Communication, my dear Second Boss,' she said. 'Communication.'

'But...' said Second Boss, feebly. 'But...' But he knew she was right. He knew he was kidding himself. He knew he was just making excuses by pretending that his EA was actually magical. He knew he was avoiding doing the thing he had to do to get the EA he wanted.

# Improve And Review

We have now identified the best way to communicate with Your EA and where you are in your working relationship. It's time to implement what you have identified to improve and review how you are working together.

## Small Changes

The little thing you can both do now is think about how you're communicating with one another. Remember that Your EA is a person just as much as she should remember that you are one too. Make allowances for each other but always employ the Four Tenets.

Focusing on developing this in your every-day working life is vital, of course, but there are other more established working practices which encourage and support effective working relationships. These practices offer perfect opportunities to practice and develop how you work together by applying your newly perfected communication skills.

Specifically I am talking about Acknowledgement of Your EA and ensuring she receives a productive Appraisal.

# Acknowledgement

## The Importance Of Thank You

I once coached an EA whose Boss had never said 'Thank You' to her. Once she almost said it but began talking to someone else to avoid any embarrassment. This was after her EA had organised the company's second Christmas party that season amidst limited budgets and constantly changing schedules.

Needless to say, that EA is no longer working for that particular Boss and now organises her spectacular parties for someone much more appreciative.

The moral of the story?

*Saying 'Thank You' means you'll never have to explain why you can't keep an EA.*

What we've talked about all the way through this book has been the need to communicate with Your EA as your Business Partner. Your EA is your sidekick, your confidante, your go-to-right-hand who has your needs as her top priority. Do you think Robin would've continued to save Batman from all those infernal circular saws and vats of acid if Batman hadn't been quite so grateful? Shouldn't your EA get some recognition of the work that she does for you? Especially when she does it so well?

Let's look at this from the other side of the coin: you do a great piece of work for your Boss. She presents this to the Board and the Board adopt your proposal without hesitation. Afterwards, she comes down to see you, tells you the good news and then heads back upstairs to the celebrations without so much as a 'ta!'. Did that make you feel like you were a valued member of a team?

## How To Say 'Thank You'

Saying 'Thank You' and meaning it is powerful. As you know, EAs can be overlooked in terms of their essential input into your success. By saying 'Thank You' you're also saying 'I respect you' - one of the four tenets of an effective relationship.

## What's In It For Me?

There aren't many things that match the warm fuzzy glow you get from thanking someone who truly deserves it. Apart from when you see a heap of kittens in a basket or a cake with your name on it. It's, quite literally, central heating for the soul.

And your EA will respond to your acknowledgement with nothing but positivity.

## Appraisals

Appraisals are the key to developing and empowering your staff, and Your EA should not be overlooked in this process.

Maybe you've had some training in giving appraisals, maybe you haven't. But let's be honest: you know how an appraisal works. You will sit with Your EA, go through her job description and her self-evaluation form and see how things are going. You will review her objectives, set some new ones and discuss what she wants to achieve over the next twelve months.

If you've already completed the Investment Process, this will be pretty easy for you to do and you'll have clear, relevant objectives already established. If the Appraisal is scheduled to take place before your *Wipe The Slate Clean Meeting* however, continue to review your EA against her existing objectives, no matter how off-message they may be after the *Wipe The Slate Clean.*

Don't use the Appraisal for a Kick-Off Meeting or even the *Wipe The Slate Clean Meeting.* This is Your EA's appraisal—any hijacking of that for your personal agenda, no matter how well-intentioned, is inappropriate.

**The Key To A Good Appraisal**

Be honest.

And by that, I don't mean be *brutally* honest. I've met EAs who have been reduced to tears every time by their Boss which indicates two things: something's clearly not right in their working relationship and that her Boss is probably a bit insensitive.

While appraisals are the place to raise any issues, any issue large enough to make someone cry should have been raised sooner. Don't wait for her appraisal to tell her that she continually misfiles your papers or that she's been calling you by the wrong name since she started (true story).

On the other hand, I've met EAs who have cried in their appraisal because their Boss has been so lovely to them. While everyone likes that kind of crying, being lovely to your EA is only good if it's true. You'll get nowhere if you're just being lovely because you don't like confrontation.

### How To Be Effectively Honest

Know what you're going to say.

A prepared appraisal is a successful appraisal. And it tends to be shorter too, if that's any incentive.

If your company doesn't have a self-evaluation element to their appraisal systems, make up one of your own. All you need is a form which asks Your EA to list her agreed objectives and to identify what's gone well and what hasn't. And while she's filling her bit in, you fill it in from your perspective too. That way, if Your EA comes in saying that her rejigging of the whole filing system was a huge success, you have your response ready if, actually, you find the new system absolutely incomprehensible.

You also get the opportunity to remember little incidents where she performed brilliantly or not quite so well and think about how you'll phrase the feedback when you're sitting in the little meeting room, eyeball-to-eyeball.

By thinking about your EA objectively you'll get a much fuller picture of what you think her achievements of the past six months or a year have been. Think about her performance in the role *as it stands now*. Make sure that you don't measure her against objectives yet to be set or a standard you have not yet told her you expect.

### A Bitter Pill?

Don't be shy of telling your EA if you think something needs work.

If she's a superstar with your clients but her timekeeping is a little whacky, tell her that. In that order. Say: 'Queenie, you are simply fabulous with my clients and you've really helped me maintain and develop my working relationships. However, I'd really like it if you could be here for 9 am each day so that we can run through the diary together.' So much easier to take a mild criticism when it's preceded by sugar. Just make sure the sugar is real and supported by as much evidence as the bitter pill.

**Developing Your EA**

Your EA is like you. She likes to grow and develop. You should think about what training or development would suit her when you're preparing for her appraisal. Do you want her to take on more project management elements of your role? What will she need to do that? Find out!

And don't forget to ask her if she needs anything. You both have a responsibility to her role and making sure that she's got all of the skills necessary to perform all of her duties. If she's struggling with Excel, there's an obvious solution...

If you are having your *Wipe The Slate Clean Meeting* within a month or so of the Appraisal, consider holding off setting objectives for the coming year until then—just ensure that this is noted on her appraisal form and whoever needs to knows to update the objectives once they have been set.

**How To Keep It In Hand**

Sometimes, if you get on well with your EA, you might end up having a little party instead of an appraisal. Or you can start making detailed plans for new projects or ways of working together.

While these are all excellent outcomes from a productive and efficient working relationship, an appraisal isn't about you. It's about your EA. It's about making sure she's clear on how she's doing in her job, where she's headed and what she needs to get there. Save the planning for a post-appraisal meeting.

## The Big No-Nos

Do not repeatedly rearrange your EA's appraisal in favour of other meetings, a late lunch or a long weekend. Your EA will feel undervalued and unimportant. Stick to the date and time you first agree together. Also, be aware that your EA may be nervous of her appraisal with you and so may be happy to rearrange. Don't give her the opportunity.

And don't ramble on when you're in there together. She hears enough of your voice during the day. This is her turn.

## In Brief

This section has focused on giving you an understanding of the importance of using Communication to establish and maintain an excellent working relationship with Your EA.

It has offered you an opportunity to understand how you communicate with Your EA and how well your working relationship is functioning through the Investment Process Part Two: The Relationship.

The stages of this process run:

- **Identify** how you communicate and how you work together. By identifying where you are, you can figure out how to move forward together. By understanding the implications of your communication style, you can figure out how to engage in a more Adult working relationship with Your EA.

- **Improve**—apply communication to improve the working relationship

- **Review**—through established business practices

By working through these stages, you will have figured out that, alongside investing in Your EA's role, investing in your relationship with Your EA will lead you to a more trusting, respectful, honest and (absolutely platonically) loving working relationship which, in turn, will result in a far more effective Business Partner.

# The Tale Of Two Bosses—Part Seven: How Second Boss Finally Got It Right

And so, after leaving profuse apologies with the King's EA, Second Boss headed straight down to his office. He called the Leader of the Land of HR and asked for a copy of the Second EA's job description to be sent up. Then, once the job description had arrived he read through it and made lots of notes about what he thought was important and what he thought was not.

Once the list was complete, he called Second EA into his office.

She scurried in and sat meekly in the chair.

'Dear Second EA,' said Second Boss. 'Are you happy in your role?'

Second EA hesitated.

'Let us get things sorted,' said Second Boss.

Second EA hesitated again and Second Boss saw her eyes begin to well.

'But first,' said Second Boss quickly. 'I want one thing agreed.' He leant forward. 'Second EA, we are equals. We are both adults. You are allowed to be assertive with me.'

'Assertive?' said Second EA, looking up. 'I can be assertive with you?'

'Yes,' said Second Boss. 'I need you to be my business partner and that means my equal.'

Silence filled the office.

'Are you okay with that?' said Second Boss suddenly racked with nerves. What if she could not? What if she would not?

Second EA swallowed and looked around the office. When her eyes returned to Second Boss he felt warm inside for they were no longer leaking or frightened. They were the eyes of someone who knew what they wanted to do.

'I...I have advanced training in all Adobe packages,' stammered Second EA. 'I think the template you're using for your tender submissions is ugly and clunky. I can do better and make it far more efficient.'

'Excellent,' said Second Boss. 'That's excellent.'

'And,' Second EA's voice was gaining in strength, indeed Second Boss had never heard her speak louder than a whisper and was impressed by this new tone. He began to feel that perhaps this was someone who could go to meetings with him. Someone who could speak with the King on his behalf without shrivelling. 'And I don't think it works that both of us are in your diary at the same time. I think we need to work out the best method to manage your meetings.'

Second EA cleared her throat.

'I agree,' said Second Boss.

'Would...would you be okay with us meeting more regularly to discuss things?'

Second Boss smiled warmly. 'I think that would work well.'

As they began to draw up a list of how they both felt they could improve and implement working practices, Second Boss looked over and saw First Boss watching him from his office. First Boss nodded and smiled. Second Boss nodded back and gave him a thumbs up.

'This is going to work,' said Second EA, smiling for the first time since she'd started working for Second Boss and forgetting all about a new job she'd been thinking about applying for all day.

And, as the sun set on the Kingdom, Second Boss and his EA worked out the best way for them to work productively, efficiently and successfully and, across the office, First Boss bought the afternoon biscuits because it was a Friday.

And they all worked as adult business partners happily, ever after.

# Moving Forward

So now you've worked through all of the processes. What next?

## Summary

Let's think about what you've learnt.

In Section One you looked at **Managing the Role of Your EA** effectively. You explored the process of defining, understanding and meeting your expectations of the role of Your EA. You did this through implementing the **Investment Process: Managing the Role**'s four simple steps:

1.  Planning

2.  Developing

3.  Implementing

4.  Reviewing

You now understand the value of defining the boundaries and priorities of Your EA's role which, in turn, also manages Your EA's expectations. You also learnt the importance of giving Your EA permission to communicate with you on an Adult-Adult basis to ensure you're working together as Business Partners and your relationship is balanced.

Section Two looked at **Managing the Relationship** which gave you an understanding of the importance of communication in establishing and maintaining the kind of working relationship you want with Your EA. You achieved this through implementing the **Investment Process: Managing the Relationship**'s three stages:

1. **Identifying** your communication styles

2. **Improving** the working relationship

3. **Reviewing** how you work together.

You have learnt that by giving it time and maintaining clear and honest communication between you and Your EA, you will have a Business Partner working with you rather than an EA working for you.

## Maintaining Your Achievement And Overcoming Stumbling Blocks

Now you've nailed how to be a great Boss and have a great working relationship with Your EA, you can't be complacent. The relationship needs to be maintained to ensure it doesn't go stale, develop an imbalance or just plain stops working.

There are three was to avoid this happening:

1. **Keep your promises**—if you said you'd meet each morning for five minutes, meet each morning for five minutes.

2. **Check-in regularly**—put regular slots in—i.e. once a month—for ten minutes where you review how things are working.

3. **Ditch what's not working**—if your five minute morning meeting isn't working, ditch it for something else that does.

## Reinvigorate And Revitalise

Have things gone off kilter a bit? Have you stopped meeting every morning? Did Your EA go on holiday and you slipped back into old habits while she was away that you're finding hard to shift now she's back? Are things spiralling out of control?

Don't panic!

It's not the end of the world if you realise that something's slipped. Gain control of it again by arranging a check-in meeting as soon as you can. Let Your EA know that you want to run through the role again with her and to revisit the plans you agreed—don't frighten her by being serious when you say this. Remember the Adult-Adult! Run through the role and plans at the meeting. Maybe something isn't quite working out as you both thought it would.

Review, reassess and reinvigorate for moving forward.

## Serious Blocks

Of course, this is the real world and things don't always run as smoothly as in the movies. You're going to come up against stumbling blocks: Your EA is uncomfortable with the Adult-Adult communication style; Your EA doesn't like change; Your EA's personality doesn't quite fit with yours.

If you're committed to the process, Your EA should come with you. She is a professional in a professional working environment and should take your investment in how you work together seriously. If you find that this isn't happening have an honest talk with her. Ask her why she can't, for example, talk to you as an Adult. Ask her what's stopping her from engaging in the process.

Perhaps you could show her this book to help her understand where you're coming from.

If you remain committed and focused and it's not working, perhaps the working relationship never will. It's okay for things not to work. It's about how you handle them when they don't. If you have serious concerns about Your EA, speak with your HR department.

# A New EA

Just as you're ambitious and want to grow, so is Your EA. That means that one day, you will come in and Your EA will be standing awkwardly by your desk with a letter in her hand and that letter will tell you she's leaving.

Of course you're happy she's moving on to better and brighter things. Your EA is marvellous, why wouldn't you want her to achieve great things?

But, equally, you're going to be sad and disappointed because you've put in so much work with her and now you'll have to start from scratch. Plus, you like Your EA—she's made your life so much easier and you'll really miss her.

What next?

1. **Get involved in the recruitment.** If company policy allows sit in on at least the second interviews for your new EA. If you're short of time or can't sit in on the interviews, review the CVs at the very least to create the shortlist. It's key that you have someone you can work with, and potentially work very well with, rather than any old bod.

2. **Implement the process as soon as Your New EA starts.** Don't wait for her to settle in—explain to her how the process goes and what you'll be working through with her. Believe me, she'll be thrilled she's got such a fantastically invested new Boss.

3. **Buy Your outgoing EA a tremendously enormous gift** to say thank you for all the hard work she has put into working for you. Jewellery normally does the trick.

# A Final Word

I hope you've enjoyed this book. I hope it's made you think, made you smile and made you really look at the role of Your EA and question: what can you do for me?

Ultimately, though, I hope that this book has changed your working life.

With commitment, focus and enthusiasm, you know how much you can achieve—look at where you are already! You owe it to yourself to have a Business Partner who will help you achieve even more.

Enjoy!

# About the Author

Susie Barron-Stubley is a highly experienced and sought after international Executive Coach, Trainer and Motivational Speaker who specialises in developing senior level Executive Assistants. She has changed the working practices of thousands of EAs around the world and has a passion, matched by few, for the professional and personal development of EAs, and enhancing how they can work proactively and productively with senior global leaders. Susie has coached many Executives alongside their Assistants in how to get the most out of the business partnership.

She is a regular traveller delivering Advanced Executive Assistant Training in Australia, China, South Africa, Dubai, India, Europe, South East Asia and the UK. This experience has given her a comprehensive global perspective on the role of senior Assistants. At home in the UK she continues to research, develop and deliver innovative and challenging development programmes to support Assistants in rapidly changing business environments to meet the expanding skill sets required of senior EAs. She is a prolific writer on the development needs of Assistants and writes for various industry publications. She was a member of the judging panel for The Times/Hays PA of the Year Awards for two years and has also produced a set of training DVDs specifically aimed at Assistants.

Susie herself spent 10 years as an Assistant before re-training as an Executive Coach and setting up Castalia Coaching & Training in early 2005 so she could use her extensive experience to support others to reach their highest potential in this challenging and complex role. She has supported high profile public figures and corporate leaders and has liaised with institutions from British Royal Households to global business executives. Her unique insight into the world of the EAs and Executives brings a distinct quality and depth to her specialist development programmes.

For further information on Susie's training courses, DVDs and books please visit the Castalia Coaching & Training website. www.castalia-training.com.

Printed in Great Britain
by Amazon.co.uk, Ltd.,
Marston Gate.